C. L. Taylor

CENSORSHIP

Richard B. Morris, Consulting Editor

Franklin Watts   1986   A First Book
New York   London   Toronto   Sydney

This book is for my parents, who have been the best of teachers and friends.

Photographs courtesy of:
New York Public Library: pp. 9, 33;
AP/Wide World: pp. 12, 48;
The Bettmann Archive: pp. 23, 26;
Reuters/Bettmann Newsphotos: p. 45;
UPI/Bettmann Newsphotos: pp. 54, 61

Library of Congress Cataloging-in-Publication Data

Taylor, C. L.
Censorship.

(A First book)
Bibliography: p.
Includes index.
Summary: Discusses the history of censorship, recent
developments and controversies, and such related issues
as freedom of speech, obscenity, libel, and intellectual
freedom.
1. Censorship—Juvenile literature. [1. Censorship]
I. Morris, Richard Brandon, 1904–   II. Title.
Z657.T29   1986   363.3′1   86-7740
ISBN 0-531-10211-4

Contents

Censorship

1

"A Drastic Effort"

Pastor Ken Bertram, of Bowie, Maryland, was determined to rid his family, his congregation, and his town of record albums, books, pamphlets, posters, T-shirts, and other items that he considered to be "poison." On October 17, 1984, Bertram and about fifty of his supporters joined in what he called a "drastic effort" to cleanse the community of the literature and music that they found offensive.

"I'm the father of four," Bertram told the crowd that had gathered in the yard of the Cornerstone Assembly of God Church. "I'm not going to sit around and watch my children take into their bodies and minds something poison and not make some kind of drastic effort to stop this."

Bertram and other members of the congregation set a small bonfire, igniting all of the materials they had gathered. These included books by Philip Roth, John Hersey, and Thomas Paine; and record albums by a variety of artists including Donny and Marie Osmond, the Beatles, Jethro Tull, Barbra Streisand, Michael Jackson, and the Rolling Stones.

This destruction of literature and other types of communication has happened many times throughout history, and continues to happen frequently today. Book burning is one example of *censorship*, which is the restriction or removal of information, or the prevention of free expression.

Censorship's many forms include cultural, political, religious, and military restrictions on spoken, written, and visual communications. These restrictions may be enforced through the establishment of laws; through the standards of publishers, producers, and various agencies; through the regulations of community groups; or through the actions of people such as Bertram and his followers, who create strong social pressure in order to see that materials they find objectionable are limited or banned. Books or parts of books may be censored, for example, as may records, television or radio programs, newspaper stories, songs, poems, plays, speeches, or movies.

The Reasons for Censorship

There are many reasons given for censorship: in a classroom or library, a book or other learning resource may be restricted or banned because it includes social, political, or religious views believed to be "inappropriate" or "threatening." A movie or television program may be considered too violent, or obscene because of nudity or "indecent" behavior. A song or speech may contain language thought to be vulgar, or ideas and values that some consider objectionable. A newspaper story may be edited or withheld from publication because it may be judged a threat to national security.

Who are the censors? Some are legislators on a local, state, or federal level. Others are members of review boards or commit-

An 1852 antislavery masterpiece, Uncle Tom's Cabin,
banned in the South, sold a million copies within a year.

tees, organized to review textbooks, films, or other forms of communication on behalf of a community. Occasionally the censors are teachers, librarians, or school administrators, who determine that a book or classroom item is not suitable for students. Often the censors are parents, members of the clergy, or other concerned citizens who worry about the presence of indecent or improper materials in their schools, libraries, theaters, book stores, and elsewhere in their community.

Censorship on the Rise

Today, censorship is reported to be on the rise throughout our society. The American Library Association, for example, whose Office for Intellectual Freedom monitors efforts to restrict access to books, announced recently that the number of reported incidents of censorship or censorship attempts at libraries has risen from three hundred in 1979 to approximately one thousand in 1984. The association publishes a monthly newsletter which documents dozens of censorship cases from around the nation.

People for the American Way, a citizens' group concerned with civil liberties, including freedom of expression, also reports a sharp increase in censorship cases in its latest annual censorship study. The report, *Attacks on the Freedom to Learn* 1984–1985, cites "a dramatic increase in censorship activity during the past school year," with "documented censorship incidents in 46 of the 50 states."

Such incidents have included the following:

• More than four hundred lines of the Shakespearean plays *Romeo and Juliet* and *Hamlet* were deleted from literature textbooks used throughout public schools in Virginia. The publisher had performed the editing without alerting teachers or school officials. It was soon discovered that other publishers had similarly cut lines from the classic dramas, because the content was thought to be inappropriate for high school readers.

• In Peoria, Illinois, parents objected to three books by contemporary writer Judy Blume: *Then Again, Maybe I Won't; Deenie;* and *Blubber.* The parents' criticisms of the books, which were located in elementary school libraries, focused on their "sexual content," "strong language," and "lack of social literary value." Two committees of school personnel recommended the removal of the books, but the school board returned them to the library. The books were restricted, however, to older students or students with the permission of their parents.

• The Southern Regional American Civil Liberties Union, in a 1984 censorship survey of public schools and libraries, reported that in Tennessee many books, including *The Diary of Anne Frank,* J. D. Salinger's *The Catcher in the Rye,* John Steinbeck's *Of Mice and Men,* and Mark Twain's *Huckleberry Finn,* had been targeted by censors. One issue of *Sports Illustrated* magazine had also been challenged. The survey reported that 37 percent of the questioned books and resources were removed from the schools.

• Books by novelists William Faulkner, Daniel DeFoe, D. H. Lawrence, Theodore Dreiser, and Judy Blume were taken from a public library exhibit in Fairfax, Virginia, and torn to shreds. Judith Anderson, the city's regional library branch manager, returned the destroyed books to the library shelves with a note stating: "Who bans books? It could be someone in your community."

"It's a depressing trend," states Barbara Parker, education policy director of People for the American Way. "It's no secret that a lot of people in this country are spending a lot of their time keeping

an eagle eye on what students read. But there's evidence that the number of self-professed censors is growing, and that the scope of their surveillance is expanding."

"Those who say that books and ideas are dangerous for our children," she continues, "—and that education should do little more than impart basic skills—seem to know little about kids, less about learning and not much about democracy."

Away from the schools and libraries, other attempts at censorship are also taking place in our society. Art exhibits have been banned from public display, for example, because they contained pieces thought to be indecent. Political and social protestors have been prevented from distributing pamphlets in public areas, such as in shopping malls or along city streets. Songs have been taken off the air by pressured radio station operators. Public speakers have been cancelled because the content of their speeches was thought to be too controversial.

Antipornography activists have targeted theaters, book stores, video shops, and other markets of obscene or offensive materials because they believe the items in question are not only without any literary or social value, but are dangerous in their portrayal of women as victims of sexual violence. The pornography issue is one of the most heated in the debate of censorship versus freedom of expression.

The boy in the photo appears to be surprised that the theater has "kiddie" matinees for "an adult film."

The Right to Free Expression

While strong cases can be made for and against different forms of censorship, many educators, lawyers, public officials, and concerned citizens worry that the rising trend of censorship in our society is a threat to our basic rights as U.S. citizens to free expression and to be informed.

At the heart of the debate is the First Amendment to the Constitution, which guarantees that our right to read, speak, write, and communicate freely cannot be obstructed by governmental interference at the state and federal levels. Certain forms of expression are not protected by this amendment, however, including libel and slander, false advertising, and obscenity.

Ours is an age in which an immeasurable amount of information is available through a range of media types: television, radio, films, newspapers, telephones, home computers, magazines, books, and so on. Along with our tremendous capability to learn and to communicate with each other, whether within our school systems or within our solar system, the complexity of the censorship issue continues to grow.

What ideas and issues should or should not be considered objectionable to what audiences in our society? Who should have censoring powers? And how does the First Amendment to the Constitution apply in the variety of censorship disputes facing our nation today?

Chapter

2

The First Amendment

"Congress Shall Make No Law . . ."

In the United States, the basic right to freedom of expression is protected from restrictive legislation by the First Amendment to the Constitution. This amendment states that:

> Congress shall make no law respecting an establishment of religion, or prohibiting the free exercise thereof; or abridging the freedom of speech, or of the press; or the right of the people peaceably to assemble, and to petition the Government for a redress of grievances.

The First Amendment is considered by many to be our most precious constitutional freedom. It is one of the ten amendments to the Constitution which together are called the Bill of Rights. Adopted in 1791, four years after the signing of the Constitution, the Bill of Rights is a declaration of basic rights of citizens. These amendments originally protected citizens' civil liberties from federal interference only. In 1925, the United States Supreme Court ruled that the states must also protect certain guarantees of the Bill of Rights, including those rights addressed in the First Amendment.

When the United States was founded, the issue of whether or not to include a bill of rights was the subject of a great debate. Many of our nation's founders, such as Thomas Jefferson and George Mason, believed that it was critical to formally declare that the civil rights of citizens would be protected from interference by the new government. These rights included freedom of speech and the press, freedom of religion, freedom of assembly, the right to bear arms, and the right to a fair arrest and to a speedy and public trial. As examples, the supporters of a bill of rights pointed to many English charters, including the English Bill of Rights of 1689, and to the states' declaration of rights in their own country, including the popular Virginia Bill of Rights of 1776.

"What the People Are Entitled To"

In drafting the Constitution, there were many arguments about including a bill of rights as part of the document. Although they agreed that the rights were important, men such as Alexander Hamilton, Patrick Henry, and Roger Sherman insisted that a federal bill of rights was unnecessary when the individual states had such bills in their own constitutions.

Opponents to the bill of rights argued further that protecting certain freedoms would be wrong when the federal government had never been granted the power to take those rights away. Hamilton stated that the bill of rights would be:

> . . . not only unnecessary in the proposed constitution, but would even be dangerous. . . . For why declare that things shall not be done which there is no power to do?

Why, for instance, should it be said that the liberty of the press shall not be restrained, when no power is given by which restrictions may be imposed?

Others argued, however, that a bill of rights was essential to the constitutional documents of a democratic nation. Jefferson stated that "A bill of rights is what the people are entitled to against every government on earth, general or particular, and what no just government should refuse or rest on inference."

Thomas Jefferson was one of the strongest proponents of the freedom of thought. He believed deeply that evil resulted from ignorance, and that progress and truth emerged from knowledge. "Error may be tolerated," he declared, "where reason is left free to combat it." Concerning freedom of the press, he once stated:

The basis of our governments being the opinion of the people, the very first object should be to keep that right; and were it left to me to decide whether we should have a government without newspapers or newspapers without government, I should not hesitate a moment to prefer the latter. But I should mean that every man should receive those papers and be capable of reading them.

Many of the state governments agreed to ratify the Constitution only with the agreement that a bill of rights would be added immediately. In order to ensure passage of the Constitution, the nation's founders generally agreed that such a bill would be addressed as one of the first orders of business for the new government.

In his inaugural address in April 1789, President George Washington stated that the bill of rights would be dealt with immediately, and in June of that year James Madison introduced the amendments to the First Congress. Twelve amendments were adopted and sent to the states for ratification. On December 15, 1791, with Virginia becoming the final state needed to ratify, ten of those amendments were formally adopted into the Constitution.

The right to free speech and press, as expressed in the First Amendment, was foremost among those included in the Bill of Rights. For many of our nation's founders, this constitutional right was reflective of the democratic republic that had been created.

Interpreting the First Amendment

Ultimately, it is the responsibility of the Supreme Court of the United States to interpret the Constitution and the Bill of Rights. Since 1791, the Court has heard many cases pertaining to the First Amendment, including cases concerning freedom of speech, freedom of the press, and the issues of libel and slander (harming someone's reputation in writing or verbally), national security, and obscenity.

Chapter

3

*Censorship Through
the Ages*

Early Forms of Censorship

Censorship has been performed by the rulers and citizens of different societies throughout the world's history. Most often, books or earlier manuscripts and other forms of communication—including poetry, sermons, speeches, and plays—have been banned because their contents were believed to conflict with the principles of a ruling church or government. More recently, within the past few hundred years, works have also been censored because they were thought to be indecent, or creating a negative influence upon readers.

In ancient Greece, as early as the fifth century B.C., the teachings of many philosophers, poets, and other writers and orators were banned because their message strayed from the culture's accepted political and religious beliefs. Socrates, a philosopher who taught that knowledge and curiosity were good and encouraged people to think for themselves, was ultimately silenced by rulers who believed that he offended the gods with his teachings. In 399 B.C., Socrates was sentenced to death by poison.

In 213 B.C., the Chinese ruler Shih Huang Ti ordered nearly all of the empire's existing manuscripts destroyed, in order to record a new history for China beginning with his rule. In so doing, Huang Ti demanded that all books describing the history and philosophies of China under its previous rulers be burned. These included many of the writings of the philosopher Confucius, who lived in the sixth century B.C.

During the Middle Ages, from approximately the year A.D. 400 into the 1400s, the Church saw that only those books in keeping with its teachings were preserved. Often, the authors of objectionable books were burned at the stake along with copies of their manuscript. These writers were considered to be "heretics," or people whose religious beliefs did not follow those of the Church.

After the introduction of mass printing in Europe in the fifteenth century, the combined Church/state government stepped up its watch over the production of literature. In 1524, Charles V of Belgium produced the first known formal list of books to be disallowed—books that were considered dangerous to the Church. In 1559, Paul IV presented the *Index Librorum Prohibitorum* (Index of Forbidden Books). The Index, which is still in existence today, has consisted of thousands of prohibited works, mostly in the areas of theology and philosophy.

England: Licensing and The Star Chamber

Both Henry VIII and Elizabeth I, rulers of England during the sixteenth and seventeenth centuries, supported the regulation of printed materials through the licensing of printers. Books that threatened the Church or government were sought out and destroyed, and their publishers were severely punished. The Star Chamber, a small court that held trials without juries and which rose to power under the reign of Charles I in the early seventeenth century, often imposed cruel punishments against printers whose books or pamphlets criticized the king.

Such strict and unfair practices in England prompted many of the country's writers to object. In 1644, John Milton condemned censorship and the practice of licensing printers in an essay entitled "Areopagitica." "Where there is much desire to learn," he wrote, "there of necessity will be much arguing, much writing, many opinions; for opinion in good men is but knowledge in the making."

Although licensing was eliminated in 1644, the English legislature passed a printing act in 1662 that condemned materials considered to be damaging or libelous to the king or the Church of England. The act forbade their production, importation, or sale.

The American Colonies

In the seventeenth and eighteenth centuries, many of the American colonies adopted restrictions similar to those enforced in England regarding the practice of religion. Many Puritans sought strict adherence to the specific doctrines of their church and did not tolerate the practice of other religions. Similarly, the Methodists and Baptists of Virginia and the Quakers of Massachusetts believed that any speech or publication that did not follow their religious ethic was blasphemous.

Others, such as Roger Williams, the founder of Rhode Island, argued that all people are entitled to choose their religious beliefs for themselves, and that they should be permitted to practice their religion freely. After finding disapproval and intolerance of his ideas in Massachusetts Bay colony, Williams and his followers left and founded the colony of Rhode Island, where he continued to uphold his theory of religious liberty. Williams's courage and determination had a great deal of influence upon many of our nation's founders. His beliefs in individual liberties are largely embodied in our constitution.

The Trial of John Peter Zenger

In 1734, a case began in the colonies against a printer named John Peter Zenger. The case would have an important impact upon the direction of free expression in the colonies, and ultimately, upon the push for the First Amendment.

Zenger printed a weekly newspaper, called the *New York Weekly Journal.* He frequently included articles in the publication that criticized the colony's British governor, William Cosby. Although many citizens agreed with Zenger's criticisms of Cosby, he was imprisoned by the colonial government, and charged with printing libelous articles.

In Zenger's defense, the prominent lawyer Andrew Hamilton addressed the jury and urged them to deliver a verdict based upon whether or not Zenger's articles contained the truth. Hamilton argued that the printer's cause—the freedom to perform an honest examination of public officials and the government—was "the best cause . . . the cause of liberty." The jury found John Peter Zenger not guilty. Hamilton was successful in his introduction of truth as an element of defense in libel cases.

The Eighteenth Century
and the Sedition Act

An emphasis on civil liberties—including freedom of expression—began to emerge in the eighteenth century, led by the teachings of Benjamin Franklin, Thomas Jefferson, and others. Legislation

In 1734 a jury found newspaper publisher
Peter Zenger not guilty of libel, and a precedent
for freedom of the press was established.

on local, state, and national levels, including the Virginia Bill of Rights and, by 1791, the First Amendment to the Constitution, emphasized freedom of speech and of the press.

In 1798, however, Congress passed a federal law that served to suppress free expression, specifically in political areas, through the threat of prosecution for seditious libel. Entitled the Sedition Act (sedition is a resistance to lawful authority), the legislation stated that it was a crime to "write, utter, or publish false, scandalous, and malicious writings or writings against the Federal government, its officials and legislators, or its laws."

The law was specifically aimed toward the many newspapers and periodicals that emerged within the latter part of the eighteenth century. These publications, largely political in nature, often featured serious criticism of the leading political party, the Federalists; of Congress; and of the president, John Adams.

Many charged that the Sedition Act was in direct violation of the First Amendment. When Thomas Jefferson became president in 1801, he pardoned those convicted under this act and returned their fines. Upon its expiration the following year, the Sedition Act was not renewed by Congress.

The states, however, continued to prosecute for seditious libel. In 1804, an editor named Harry Croswell was accused of seditious libel for remarks he had published about Thomas Jefferson. Alexander Hamilton, presenting Croswell's defense, closely followed the case as presented by Andrew Hamilton in the trial of John Peter Zenger seventy years before.

Hamilton urged the court to consider the cause of freedom of the press, and to weigh the factor of truth as a defense. Croswell was acquitted, and the following year New York adopted a bill that permitted truth as a defense in libel cases, if the truth were published "with good motives and for justifiable ends."

The Threat to Abolitionist Papers

Prior to the Civil War, in the early to mid-nineteenth century, many editors began to publish pamphlets and newspapers that demanded the freedom of the slaves in the South, and called for the complete abolition of slavery in the United States. The debate over this issue became quite heated throughout our nation.

Many times during this period, the print shops, offices, and equipment of the abolitionist publishers were destroyed by pro-slavery groups and individuals. In at least one instance, the furor and determination to censor the antislavery publications resulted in murder: Elijah Parish Lovejoy, editor of an abolitionist newspaper entitled the *Philanthropist*, was killed while trying to prevent an angry mob from destroying his printing press.

The First Obscenity Cases

With the nineteenth century came the first cases to be tried against books and materials charged with being obscene. In 1821, Vermont became the first state (with many others to follow) to pass a state antiobscenity law; and in Massachusetts, the book *Fanny Hill* became the first to be banned by a state because it was judged to be obscene.

The first federal antiobscenity law was the Tariff, or customs, Law of 1842. This law limited the importation of indecent or obscene materials, including prints, paintings, lithographs, and engravings. In 1865, Congress prohibited the passage of obscene materials through the U.S. mails.

In England, the Cockburn ruling of 1868 had a large influence upon the course of obscenity cases on both sides of the Atlantic Ocean for many years. Here, in the *Hicklin* case, Judge Cockburn

COMSTOCK'S NEXT MOVE—PROBABLY.

Some found amusement in Anthony Comstock's actions
as censor of public and private behavior.

ruled that "the test of obscenity is this: whether the tendance of the matter charged as obscenity is to deprave and corrupt those into whose hands a publication of this sort may fall." This decision prompted the concept that citizens needed to be protected from indecent or corrupt literature.

Comstockery!

In the 1860s, a crusader for censorship named Anthony Comstock began his campaign against obscenity in the state of New York. In 1872, he teamed up with the state's Young Men's Civic Association (YMCA), and formed the Committee for the Suppression of Vice. A year later, Comstock became the Secretary of the New York Society for the Suppression of Vice, and was then permitted by the state to make arrests.

Comstock was strongly opposed to literature he believed to be indecent, and he sought to rid society of obscene books, magazines, and plays. He wanted not only to see the materials destroyed and their merchants arrested; he wanted to prosecute the publishers as well. He also attempted to shut down saloons and night clubs, which he believed to be the promoters of indecent behavior.

In 1873, partly in response to the pressures of Comstock and his followers, Congress toughened the Mail Act of 1865, broadening the range of materials that could be classified as obscene and therefore nonmailable. The Federal Obscenity Act, otherwise known as the Comstock Act, thus allowed for liberal censorship of literature. Comstock was named a special agent to the Post Office in connection with this act, and he attacked his duties vigorously.

Comstock's movement to "clean up" the nation had a powerful effect that spread throughout the states. Many states adopted strict antiobscenity laws. Other powerful societies against the suppression of vice, including the New England Watch and Ward Society, also arose in the latter part of the century. Comstock's notoriety prompted the famous playwright George Bernard Shaw, whose works Comstock had attempted to censor, to coin the term "Comstockery!" in referring to censorship.

The Court Cases of the Twentieth Century

The intense guard against obscenity, which had largely been provoked by Comstock and his supporters, lasted through the early part of the twentieth century. In 1913, however, a case brought before a federal court, and the resulting remarks of Judge Learned Hand, served as an indication that the trend was beginning to taper off.

The defendant in the case was a publisher named Mitchell Kennerly. Anthony Comstock, after reading a novel that Kennerly had published and that Comstock found objectionable, had him arrested. Judge Hand convicted Kennerly, because the law was so clear in its definition of obscenity, but he questioned the rigidity of the law, and pointed out that views of obscenity could—and had—changed with the times.

Many books were brought before the federal courts on obscenity charges during the first half of the twentieth century. These books included many classics that had been written and published abroad but were not permitted to be imported to or published within the United States. Among these works were Theodore Dreiser's *An American Tragedy*, Voltaire's *Candide*, and D. H. Lawrence's *Lady Chatterly's Lover*.

In 1933, Random House Publishers of New York initiated one of the most significant such court cases. The book in question was *Ulysses*, by the Irish writer, James Joyce. The book had been published in Paris; however, when a copy was sent to New York for printing in New York, it was halted at customs.

Federal Court Judge John M. Woolsey cleared the novel of the obscenity charges, and thus permitted its entry and publication within the United States. Judge Woolsey determined that the book was indeed a significant work of art, and that when the book was viewed as a whole, it could not be considered indecent. "I hold that 'Ulysses' is a sincere and honest book," Woolsey wrote, adding:

> If one does not wish to associate with such folk as Joyce describes, that is one's own choice. In order to avoid indirect contact with them one may not wish to read "Ulysses"; that is quite understandable. But when such a real artist in words, as Joyce undoubtably is, seeks to draw a true picture of the lower middle class in a European city, ought it to be impossible for the American public legally to see that picture?

Despite the advances against literary censorship that resulted from Judge Woolsey's decision, especially from his statements on the necessity of viewing a book by its entire contents and not by a few isolated passages, the issues surrounding the definition of obscenity remained cloudy. Two Supreme Court decisions—the *Roth* decision in 1957 and the *Miller* case in 1973–served to clarify the subject somewhat, although today the definition is still widely debated.

In the case of *Roth* versus *the United States*, the Supreme Court examined the constitutionality of antiobscenity laws for the first time. The court ruled that obscene materials were indeed not protected by the First Amendment. The justices were careful, however, to point out that there were limitations to what could and could not be defined as obscene: ". . . Sex and obscenity are not synonymous. . . . The portrayal of sex, e.g., in art, literature and scientific works, is not itself sufficient reason to deny material the constitutional protection of freedom of speech and press." They emphasized that modern community standards must be applied when judging the works in question, and that, again, the works must be evaluated as a whole, not in part.

Miller versus *California* is the most recent court case which has examined the definition of obscenity in the United States. Marvin Miller was convicted of distributing obscene materials through the mails. He appealed the case on the grounds that the state's antiobscenity law was unconstitutional. Upon reaching the Supreme Court, the court upheld the constitutionality of state obscenity laws, but ruled that the scope of those laws must be very limited.

The court rejected the theory that a national definition of obscenity must apply, ruling instead that community standards should serve as guidelines. The work may also be banned only if it lacks "serious literary, artistic, political or scientific value."

Censorship, when examined in terms of the very complex issue of obscenity, continues to be a subject of current debate. Similarly, as our nation's knowledge and technology continue to develop, many other issues arise concerning the freedom of information and of expression. Just as in the days when Socrates stirred up controversy through his speeches in ancient Greece, or when John Peter Zenger angered the British government in the eighteenth century, censorship is a widely argued concern in the 1980s. The debate takes place in our courts, schools, libraries, newsrooms, book stores, theaters, and in many other corners of our society.

4

Information and Enlightenment

The Freedom to Read

Each September, many U.S. organizations who are concerned with the rising threat of censorship in our society sponsor "Banned Books Week." In 1985, the theme for Banned Books Week was "Free Speech/Free Press," and sponsoring organizations, who include the American Library Association, the American Booksellers Association, and the Association of American Publishers, reminded citizens of the many writers who have been (or are still) the targets of censors. Among these writers are William Shakespeare, Mark Twain, Alexander Solzhenitsyn, James Baldwin, and Judy Blume.

The organizations also pointed out that library censorship is at an all-time high. Many books have been the "victims" of people who, either acting alone or as part of a group, have complained and requested the books' removal or restriction. Often, books, periodicals, record albums, and videotapes have disappeared from libraries at the hands of self-appointed censors. Many materials have been destroyed.

People who censor books argue that their actions are in the "best interest" of all people. They choose to censor for many different reasons: they believe that the books are indecent, or contain vulgar language; the photographs or illustrations are "dirty"; the stories are too violent, or present crime in a positive way; or the ideas included are immoral or unpatriotic or simply without value. Others censor because they believe that a certain group of people (women, blacks, or Jews, for example) are treated poorly or unfairly in a book. Not only is there a growing and varied number of reasons for finding books objectionable; today, more and more people are willing to voice—and take action upon—their objections.

But many others—librarians, educators, legislators, writers, publishers, and students among them—believe in following the tradition of our First Amendment. They point out that this tradition allows us the freedom to read, write, speak, and therefore to think and learn; and that this freedom is essential to a progressive, inventive society. They also believe that it is impossible to ever agree upon what should be censored and what should not: by whose standards shall restrictions be set? And who will censor the censors?

The Library Bill of Rights

"Library materials shall be chosen for values of interest, information, and enlightenment of all the people in the community." According to the American Library Association's (ALA) Library Bill of Rights, that is the objective of our nation's librarians, both within our communities and our schools. Originally drafted in 1948, the bill continues, "censorship shall be challenged by libraries in the maintenance of their responsibility to provide public information and enlightenment." These policies are based upon the First Amendment to the Constitution.

The main reading room of
the New York Public Library

Since 1940, the American Library Association has monitored cases of attempts to ban or restrict library books, through its Committee on Intellectual Freedom. As further stated in the ALA's Bill of Rights, the Association's goal is to protect "the free access to ideas and full freedom of expression that are the tradition and heritage of Americans."

The ALA is joined in their efforts to uphold First Amendment tradition by many other organizations, including the National Council of Teachers of English (NCTE). In its Statement of Concern, issued by the NCTE's Committee Against Censorship, the organization points to the "steady erosion of First Amendment rights," adding that they are "united in the conviction that censorship of what we see and hear and read constitutes an unacceptable dictatorship over our minds and a dangerous opening to religious, political, artistic and intellectual repression."

The NCTE further points out that:

> The American public schools, for many years, have been faced with the problem of censorship. Many such problems have been fostered by groups who question the use of instructional materials that do not meet their moral, religious, political, cultural or ethnic values. . . . These groups constantly remind the profession that they are the persons who "pay the bill" for the operation of schools; therefore, they have the right to make final decisions as to what curricular materials should be selected and used in *their* schools.

The freedom to read is at the heart of the censorship debate. Our public libraries and our schools, therefore, have become the battlegrounds for this heated issue.

The Case in Kanawha County

In April 1974, Alice Moore, a school board member in Kanawha County, West Virginia, announced her objections to over three hundred different textbooks that had been submitted to the board by a local textbook selection committee. The texts, which had all been approved by the state, were part of a new language-arts program planned for the county's schools.

Mrs. Moore claimed that the books were unsuitable for use in the schools, charging that they contained filthy language, unpatriotic ideas, and concepts that were in contradiction to the Christian faith. The school board voted, however, to allow the new texts to be taught in the schools, by a vote of three to two.

By the time the schools opened in September of that year, Mrs. Moore and many community supporters, including church officials, had organized a boycott. They kept their children out of the schools, and staged pickets and demonstrations. Soon the episode escalated into a violent and dangerous situation with shootings and bombings, forcing the schools to close.

A committee of citizens was organized by the school board to carefully review the texts. Several weeks later, the special committee recommended that the books continue to be used in the schools. They added that no child would be required to read them, if a parent objected.

Mrs. Moore and her supporters believed that the study of the texts would be damaging to their children's education and upbringing. They believed that not only their children but all children in their community should be protected from literature that they found offensive. But other parents, teachers, school administrators, church officials, and a majority of the school board disagreed, as did the eighteen-member committee that made the final decision regarding the texts.

The incident in Kanawha County, which left the community bitter and sharply divided, received a great deal of national attention. It became very clear that this was a critical issue that people took very seriously; that the issue could arise at any time in any community; and that it was extremely difficult to attempt to resolve the issue to everyone's liking.

Protests:
From Dickens to Anne Frank

Within recent years, many such cases of censorship have emerged within public and private schools throughout our nation. Textbooks, literature, films, posters, videos, brochures, comic strips, and other materials have become the subjects of protests. Even novels considered to be classics and frequently taught in the classroom have been the targets of censors. These books include Charles Dickens's *Oliver Twist*; George Orwell's *1984* and *Animal Farm*; Pearl Buck's *The Good Earth*; Ernest Hemingway's *The Sun Also Rises*; *The Diary of Anne Frank*; and John Steinbeck's *The Grapes of Wrath* and *Of Mice and Men*.

The levels and types of censorship in the schools vary. Occasionally, a parent may object to his or her child reading a particular book in class, and will express concern to the child's teacher. In this case, the teacher will often suggest an alternate reading assignment for the student. Similarly, a parent may request that books be restricted in the school library. For example, books may be reserved for only the older children within the school, or only those children with parental permission.

Certainly, the most bold form of censorship is direct book banning. In this instance, a book may fall into the hands of a parent or member of a community who believes the book to be unacceptable for schoolchildren. That person may respond by demanding that the book be removed completely from the classrooms or library shelves. Frequently, a school board will then meet to discuss and resolve the issue.

Island Trees

Another recent episode of censorship in the public schools took place in the Island Trees Union Free School District in Long Island, New York. The district's board of education voted to remove nine books from the school libraries, including works by Kurt Vonnegut, Eldridge Cleaver, and Bernard Malamud—on grounds that the books were offensive, obscene, and/or violent.

Several students and their parents, together with the New York Civil Liberties Union, filed a lawsuit against the school board to protest the withdrawal of the books. The first court decision went in favor of the school board. In a court of appeals, however, it was decided that there should be a trial to examine the case. Next, the U.S. Supreme Court stepped in, and in June 1982, announced its agreement that there should be a trial.

The Supreme Court determined that the school board's motives in removing the books needed to be explored, adding: "We think that the First Amendment rights of students may be directly and sharply implicated by the removal of books from the shelves of a school library. . . . [W]e hold that local school boards may not remove books from school library shelves simply because they dislike the ideas contained in those books. . . ."

The court also ruled that a school board *may* act to remove books if they are believed to be "educationally unsuitable" or "vulgar." The actions of the Island Trees district school board were to be reevaluated under this criteria.

Following the Supreme Court's decision in *Island Trees*, however, it remained unclear what kind of constitutional guidelines were to be followed by school boards in their book-selection policies. The selection of textbooks and library materials is a complex procedure, and often raises the question of preselection censorship by state and local boards. Furthermore, in yet another dimension of textbook censorship, it has recently been discovered that the textbook publishers themselves may have a hand in censoring what our nation's students read.

"An America Without Hamburgers"

"Honest Injun!" is a favorite expression of Tom, the lovable but mischievous hero of Mark Twain's *Tom Sawyer*. But "Honest Injun" and many other such slang and colloquial expressions were edited from "The Glorious Whitewasher" chapter when it appeared in a recently published sixth-grade literature textbook. The phrases were either deleted or replaced with grammatically correct language.

This example of "doctoring" literature and other subject matter for students reflects a national trend among major U.S. textbook publishers. Late in 1984, the Virginia Board of Education made its discovery that texts of Shakespeare and other classics had been edited by publishers, resulting in the deletion of hundreds of lines from *Romeo and Juliet* and *Hamlet*. That discovery prompted the educators to appeal to publishers to either present the literary works in full, or clearly indicate to teachers where the text had been altered.

"The Virginia Board of Education determined that at least 35 percent of all textbooks used in the state's public high schools in the past year had been censored or 'dumbed down' by publishers concerned that the texts were boring or not readable in the unabridged version," states Margaret S. Marston, a member of the state board. She cites other examples:

> "Unalienable," for example, was eliminated for unknown reasons before the word "rights" in one publisher's version of the Declaration of Independence. One textbook publisher changed the title of a story called "A Perfect Day for Ice Cream" to "A Perfect Day" and eliminated a central trip to an ice cream parlor because it seemed to advocate junk food. For first graders, "The Shoemaker and the Elves" was rewritten so that in one version the words "elves," "shoemaker" and even "shoes" never appear.

Anthony Podesta, of People for the American Way, points out that parents should examine textbooks closely today, because prepublication censorship is resulting in a lack of challenging material for students:

> Take a look at the books your children are assigned in school. You'll find attractive pictures and eye-catching graphics. You'll also find short words, short sentences, short paragraphs, and short chapters. In a nutshell, many textbooks are short on substantive information that challenges students to think for themselves. Too many textbooks are inadequate because they were written not to promote learning, but to avoid controversy.

Elsa Walsh, a *Washington Post* writer, also points out that "text-books mention many subjects without focusing on any in depth." She adds that parents and educators are beginning to question and criticize texts, because "the America that students read about is often not the America of their neighborhoods or schoolyards. It is an America without hamburgers or family conflict, a history without cowboys and Indians. . . ."

As an example, Walsh cites that "In one chapter on national government in a popular fifth-grade social studies book . . . more space is devoted to the structure and décor of the White House than to the workings of the legislative branch and more detail is provided about the Capitol building than the job of the president."

Textbook publishers, however, argue that the pressure against them to edit and precensor texts is very high. They point to powerful organizations and state and local educators who have influence in the decisions as to which textbooks are selected within their school systems. Twenty-two states have established boards to review texts on a regular basis. Other states rely upon independent agencies, in addition to local schoolboards, to review and approve texts.

In the state of Texas, for example, groups such as Educational Research Analysts review all textbooks under consideration for the state's schools. As one of the nation's leading purchasers of texts, Texas has a large amount of influence upon what publishers print, and as a result, upon what our nation's students read.

Educational Research Analysts is clear about its position against introducing complex subjects—such as sex education, nuclear warfare, the study of drug or alcohol abuse, or the theory of evolution—in classrooms. Similarly, the organization is disapproving of introducing topics such as women's rights, civil rights, or environmentalism. They will not approve materials that challenge students to make their own decisions about such subjects, stating that "Allowing a student to come to his own conclusions about concepts creates confusion."

But Margaret Marston and other educators disagree: "We are reducing the challenge to our students to think about the complex world in which they live." She urges that "teachers be given the freedom to conduct balanced discussions of important social and political issues. . . . The challenges and complexities of our world call for keen thinkers and competent thinkers."

Bill Honig, Superintendent of Public Instruction for California state schools, agrees. Recently, the State Board of Education rejected all twenty-nine junior high school science textbooks that had been submitted for approval. Honig pointed out that the texts, which had been submitted by eight different publishers, were "watered down," and did not adequately address important topics, such as the theory of evolution.

Honig stresses that it is important for students to have books that are "engaging and challenging," adding that "It turns out that children can read at a lot higher level if you give them interesting stories. . . . They should be taught the best wisdom of our civilization."

Chapter

5

Art or Obscenity?

"My *one* regret about the era in which I made films was the lack of
freedom to be honest. . . . Censorship . . . hurt the honesty of
our performances." Bette Davis, award-winning film and stage star,
is critical of the many years of filmmaking—from the 1930s into
the 1960s—in which the threat of a censor's poor rating was a
source of extreme discouragement for the industry's actors, writers,
directors, and producers.

Monitoring the Movies

Censorship of the movies dates almost as far back as the appearance
of the first silent movie in 1905. The film industry itself and national, state, and community agencies have monitored and rated
films, with the ratings often serving as indicators of a film's success
or failure. Films judged to be suitable for adults and children alike
received mild ratings, while those films found to be "morally dangerous" by review boards received low ratings, and often became
box-office failures.

The motion picture industry began its own production code in 1930, thus establishing standards of decency for U.S. filmmakers to follow. In 1934, the National Legion of Decency of the Catholic Church began to review films, applying ratings on the basis of moral standards. These ratings had a much stronger influence on filmmaking than the industry's own code, and films were often edited and reworked to raise their ratings.

Films fell into four classifications, according to the National Legion of Decency. The "A-1" category was reserved for films that were suitable for all viewers. "A-2" meant that the film required maturity of its viewers, and was probably not suitable for children. The "B" classification was for films that contained some elements (strong language, nudity, sex, or violence) that were not appropriate for everyone. "C" meant that the film was "condemned," or "positively bad."

These ratings were widely respected by American viewers for several decades. The threat of a "C" rating had a powerful effect upon filmmakers, and resulted in the elimination of many "questionable" scenes from films of the era. As an example, Rhett Butler's classic parting line to Scarlett O'Hara in the 1939 epic, *Gone With the Wind*, was nearly dropped from the film. "Frankly, my dear, I don't give a damn" was considered a very risky line of dialogue, but producer David Selznick insisted that it remain.

Today, restrictions upon what may be shown in a film are far more relaxed, and filmmakers are freer to include controversial subjects, coarse language, nudity, sex, crime, and violence. State and local obscenity laws do apply to films, but very few communities have established boards that regularly review films.

Audiences rely instead upon the Motion Picture Code and Rating Program, established by the Motion Picture Association of

America in 1968. These ratings are given to all films submitted to the Association for review, and serve as guidelines used by moviegoers to predetermine the contents of a film. Ratings, after some refining by the Association, are now listed as: "G," for general audiences; "PG," suggesting that parental guidance may be necessary; "PG 13," indicating that the film may not be suitable for viewers under the age of thirteen; "R," for restricted audiences over the age of seventeen unless accompanied by an adult; and "X," meaning no one under the age of eighteen may be permitted.

As is the case with other communication mediums, the consumer—in this case, the moviegoer—also possesses powerful influence and the ability to censor. When angry parents in Milwaukee, Wisconsin, organized Citizens Against Movie Madness in November 1984 to protest a violent horror movie being shown in their neighborhood, the film was removed from the local theaters. Shortly afterward, in response to the national attention that the parents' organization received, the film was withdrawn from theaters across the nation.

Similar protests by community members have resulted in the removal of pornographic films from neighborhood theaters, and in some cases theaters have been shut down in response to negative pressures. Such efforts, coupled with efforts of the movie industry

In the United States, as in France, the showing of Je vous salue, Marie *(in English,* Hail, Mary) *was opposed in some places as sacrilegious and was stopped.*

to regulate itself, demonstrate the demand upon filmmakers to be sensitive to the opinions of viewers.

The Evolution of Television Programming

According to a recent survey, television is present in more American homes than either telephones or indoor plumbing. Adults watch an average of four to six hours of television per day; for children, that is a minimum. The most influential of all communication mediums, television is also among the most censored.

As the lifestyles, values, and attitudes of Americans have changed over the years, so has television programming. Beginning with its explosive popularity in the 1950s, television has been used as a means of entertainment, information, education, influence, and protest medium. Yet much of what is acceptable today would not have been attempted on television thirty years ago.

Soap operas, for example, are far more explicit today in their scenes of affection and lovemaking. Crime shows include realistic scenes of violence unheard of in the early days of television. Strong language has become more acceptable in comedy routines and dramas. Many of these changes in television standards caused community action groups in April 1976 to pressure television networks to establish "family viewing time". Family viewing time sets aside early evening hours for programs considered to be suitable for the entire family.

Although television has grown more permissive in program content, it is still heavily impacted by the influence of the advertising market, which, in turn, is influenced by television viewers. If viewers find a program offensive, and discontinue watching it as a result, advertisers lose viewers for their commercials. When a program loses the support of advertisers, it is not likely to last in the television line-up.

Television and radio stations are not subject to direct regulating powers concerning programming content, although they are sensitive to the opinions of viewers, community action groups, and advertisers. In addition, the Federal Communications Commission (FCC) takes into account the "public interest" in a station's programming when granting and renewing operating licenses. If the FCC determines that a station has a history of airing questionable programs, it may not renew the station's license.

Another aspect of control upon television and radio stations, administered by the FCC, is the Fairness Doctrine. The Fairness Doctrine, established in 1967, requires that broadcasters devote equal time to discussions of both sides of political issues. Originally drafted to ensure that viewers and listeners were able to learn both sides of a controversial issue, many broadcasters today support the repeal of the Fairness Doctrine. They point out that while the policy served its purpose when there were only a few stations, today, with the success of cable television, there are a variety of stations to choose from and viewers are easily able to learn many different points of view.

Labeling the Lyrics

The power of consumers to influence and regulate the recording industry was demonstrated recently in a debate over whether or not to label lyrics on rock music albums that might be considered offensive. Two parents' groups—the Parents Music Resource Center and the national Parent-Teacher Association—had expressed concern about the lyrics on many popular rock albums. "Some of

these lyrics reinforce all the wrong kinds of values for children at a very tender age," observed Susan Baker, of the Parents Music Resource Center.

After months of negotiation with members of the recording industry, the parents' groups came away with an important compromise: on albums with lyrics involving sex, violence, or drug or alcohol abuse, the record companies will place either a warning label (stating "Explicit Lyrics—Parental Advisory") on the jacket, or they will print the lyrics on the back cover or on lyric sheets.

Musicians and other members of the recording industry were cautious about taking such measures, warning that such restrictions constituted censorship and would limit creative freedoms protected by the First Amendment. They pointed out that such measures were no substitute for parental guidance. The Recording Industry Association of America stated, however, that the labeling is "intended to respond sensitively to the concerns of parents of younger children and to achieve a fair balance with the essential rights and freedoms of creators, performers, and adult purchasers of recorded music."

The new policies adopted by the recording industry again reflect the influence of the concerned consumer. Freedom of expression, however, deserves at least "a fair balance," and the dispute over ratings and labels for rock albums served as another indication of the sensitive, complicated nature of the censorship issue.

Groups of parents disapprove of the "explicit lyrics" of some of the songs recorded by rock groups and stars like Prince.

Chapter

6

The Flow of Information:
Freedom of the Press

In 1735, when the jury in John Peter Zenger's trial found him not guilty of printing seditious libel, an important step had been taken toward securing freedom of the press in this country. The founders of the United States government carried through on protecting this liberty by assuring a free press in the First Amendment to the Constitution.

As Richard J. V. Johnson, chairman and president of the American Newspaper Publishers Association, commented recently:

> More than 200 years ago we inherited much of our law and our customs from the British. But they had no free press. The free press concept was born when America was born. It wasn't handed down or inherited. It was deliberately structured in the spirit of independence as absolutely crucial to the creation and maintenance of a free society.

Today, both citizens and government officials alike continue to respect and rely upon the freedom of the press, which includes newspapers, news magazines, and television and radio programs. But a great deal of responsibility accompanies that freedom; specifically, the responsibility of the reporter to make an honest attempt to record the news fairly and truthfully. Difficult questions, such as how to balance the right to complete news coverage versus the issues of national security and libel, continue to confront our news media, and serve as reminders that the press in the United States can indeed be challenged and controlled.

The Issue of Libel

Several twentieth-century court cases have attempted to provide clear and narrow definitions of libel, with the intent of limiting the restrictions upon the press in this area. In a 1931 Supreme Court case, *Near* versus *Minnesota*, the court ruled as unconstitutional a state statute which forbade "malicious, scandalous and defamatory" newspapers or periodicals. This case centered around a Minneapolis newspaper that regularly criticized local law-enforcement officers. In ruling against the statute, which would have prohibited such reporting, the court pointed out that such a law was, in effect, censorship because it suppressed freedom of the press.

The Supreme Court further attempted to clarify and strengthen freedom of the press in its 1964 ruling in the case of *New York Times Company* versus *Sullivan*. In this case, the *New York Times* newspaper had been sued for running a paid advertisement that spoke against the poor treatment of blacks in Montgomery, Alabama. The Montgomery police commissioner, among others, argued that the advertisement contained inaccuracies that were libelous, and an Alabama court ruled in his favor.

The Supreme Court unanimously reversed that judgment. The

justices held that in libel cases pertaining to public figures, certain allowances must be made to insure and protect the constitutional right to freedom of speech and the press.

The court went on to declare, however, that a libel case would be possible if a false statement in question were made with "actual malice," or "with knowledge that it was false or with reckless disregard of whether it was false or not." In the case at hand, the court ruled that malice could not be proved against the *New York Times*. With this ruling, the Supreme Court upheld the protection of the free press, but as has been demonstrated in recent cases, the court also cleared the way for libel cases based upon the 1964 definitions.

Two recent libel cases that received national attention were brought by General William Westmoreland against the CBS television network, and by Ariel Sharon, former defense minister of Israel, against *Time* magazine. In both cases, the men charged that the news media had libeled them through the deliberate misrepresentation of facts.

Although the cases against the media were dismissed in both instances, the trials raised many questions about the reporting practices of members of the news media. On the other hand, if extreme precautionary measures must be taken before a story is printed, to insure absolute fairness and accuracy, how much freedom is left to our journalists to report the news as quickly and responsively as possible?

A 1985 survey conducted by the American Society of Newspaper Editors revealed that the public does have many reservations about the accuracy and fairness of newspaper reporting. Newspaper columnist Nick Thimmesch, of the *Richmond Times-Journal*, points out, however, that although the "survey shows that the public does indeed have many dark views of newspapers," readers "salute papers for uncovering evil, pursuing vice, maintaining patriotism and morality, and genuinely working for the community's well-being."

The Press and National Security

National security and the protection of freedom of the press is an issue that has arisen many times in the history of our country, frequently during wartime. At what point may our top-level government officials decide that information should not be available through the media because it may damage our national security? Should our journalists, if they have gained access to sensitive information, be relied upon to decide whether it is in the public interest to be openly informed of secret government activities?

This question was brought before our nation in the 1971 Pentagon Papers case. A government employee named Daniel Ellsberg gave the *New York Times* copies of a Pentagon report that contained classified information about U.S. actions in Vietnam. The *Times* began to print the Pentagon Papers, but the government promptly demanded that the newspaper halt publication and return the papers.

The *Times* refused to stop printing excerpts from the papers, and a legal battle began between the federal government and the press which finally arrived in the Supreme Court. The court ruled that the *Times*'s publication of the Pentagon Papers was indeed protected by the First Amendment. Justice Hugo Black stated:

In the First Amendment the Founding Fathers gave the free press the protection it must have to fulfill its essential role in our democracy. The press was to serve the governed, not the governors. The Government's power to censor the press was abolished so that the press would

Daniel Ellsberg and his wife, Patricia, after the dismissal
of his case in connection with the Pentagon Papers

remain forever free to censure the Government. The press was protected so that it could bare the secrets of government and inform the people.

Recently, the complexity of the free press versus national security debate was illustrated in the instance of the United States invasion of the island of Grenada. When U.S. forces invaded the island in October 1983, reporters were prevented by the government from covering the action for close to forty-eight hours. A few reporters who had managed to land upon Grenada by fishing boat were evacuated immediately by helicopter, and were not permitted to file stories with their newspapers.

In addition, reporters at home were given no information by the White House—in fact, they were told that such an invasion of Grenada was "preposterous." When the truth became known, many questions were raised about the government's decision to keep the media—and therefore the public—in the dark.

Many argued that at least providing minimal information to the public would have served to reduce its fears, especially since the public was found to be largely supportive of the invasion afterward. Government officials, however, including defense secretary Caspar Weinberger, maintained that utmost secrecy was essential to the success of the defense operation.

Such instances of the press clashing with the efforts of government prompted President John F. Kennedy to state, "In times of clear and present danger, the courts have held that even the privileged rights of the First Amendment must yield to the public's need for national security." An October 28, 1983, editorial from the *Washington Post* states, however, "If the American media can be excluded by their own government from direct coverage of events of great importance to the American people, the whole character of the relationship between governors and governed is affected."

"A Unique Right"

The news media in our country has an indispensable—and widely regarded—function in keeping the public informed of events at the local, state, national, and international level. The media's task of monitoring governmental activities, and informing the public regularly of current policies, actions, statements, goals, and motives of government officials, is essential to this role.

According to Richard J. V. Johnson, "As citizens we must continually remind ourselves that freedom of the press is a unique right of the American people and that it is indeed the American people's freedom. . . ."

"Above all," he continues, "we must never forget that a free press is crucial to the preservation of all of the freedoms embodied in our Constitution. Once we lose it, the other precious freedoms we enjoy will crumble."

Chapter

7

Voices Speaking Out

In many countries, freedom of expression is extremely limited or simply not permitted. In these societies, the government often censors views that are not in keeping with its policies, disallowing controversial opinions to be aired on television, in a newspaper, in a public speech, or even in a private meeting.

This often includes the opinions of the nation's news reporters and publishers, and of its poets, writers, philosophers, actors, musicians, teachers, and ministers. Citizens who have grievances about their government, who question their leaders, or who voice independent views without prior government approval may be subject to severe punishment: fines and imprisonment, exile from their countries, or possibly death.

Entrusting the American People

Our country's founding documents, and specifically the First Amendment, were drafted to protect the rights of all American citizens to both question and criticize the government, if they wish. Our founders believed that with many voices speaking out, truth would always emerge, and our country would prosper as a fair and free nation.

President John F. Kennedy echoed these beliefs when he said:

> We are not afraid to entrust the American people with unpleasant facts, foreign ideas, alien philosophies, and competitive values. For a nation that is afraid to let its people judge the truth and falsehood in an open market is a nation that is afraid of its people.

Throughout our nation's history, however, citizens have questioned how much power our government *does* have in controlling the flow of information—what we say, publish, hear, and read. In many ways, our government is able to restrict information and ideas. For example, government officials and employees may label certain types of information "classified" or top secret. Documents likely to be censored include publications on sensitive subjects such as defense technology, or certain scientific discoveries.

Other methods of governmental censorship include limiting what present and former government employees may speak and write about, or refusing to allow some foreign scholars into our country and limiting foreign publications. During wartime, the restrictions on free expression have become even stricter, in an effort to insure national security.

National Security and the World Wars

During World War I, Congress passed laws with the objective of censoring news reporting and other forms of communication in an effort to protect the nation. These laws included the Espionage Act, the Trading With The Enemy Act, and the Sedition Act.

The Espionage Act, passed in June 1917, was enacted to prevent disloyalty and the obstruction of military recruitment. The law prohibited publications containing such information from being mailed.

Passed by Congress in October 1917, the Trading With The Enemy Act required that publishers of newspapers and magazine articles that were written in a foreign language file sworn translations with local postmasters. The Sedition Act of May 1918 prohibited writing or publishing "any disloyal, profane, scurrilous or abusive language about the form of government of the United States. . . ."

The Clear and Present Danger Test

Under the 1917 Espionage Act, the case of *Schenck* versus *the United States* was brought before the Supreme Court. The court upheld a lower court's decision that the distribution during wartime of pamphlets that spoke against the military draft was dangerous. Speaking for the court, Judge Oliver Wendell Holmes said:

> We admit that in many places and in ordinary times the defendants in saying all that was said in the circular would have been within their constitutional rights. But the character of every act depends upon the circumstances in which it was done. . . . The most stringent protection of free speech would not protect a man in falsely shouting fire in a crowded theatre and causing a panic. . . . The question in every case is whether the words used are used in such circumstances and are of such a nature as to create a clear and present danger that they will bring about the substantive evils that Congress has a right to

prevent. It is a question of proximity and degree. When a nation is at war many things that might be said in time of peace are such a hindrance to its efforts that their utterance will not be endured so long as men fight and that no court could regard them as protected by any constitutional right.

In a 1919 Supreme Court case, *Abrams* versus *the United States*, Holmes added that he believed that this type of governmental censorship should only apply when the act is "immediately dangerous." In the *Abrams* case, the act in question was the distribution of pamphlets that spoke against the American government's sending troops to Russia in 1918. The Russian immigrants who had produced the pamphlets also urged a strike of American munitions workers. The call for such a strike while America was at war constituted an immediate danger according to the Court's majority, and the conviction was upheld.

In 1940, prior to United States involvement in World War II, Congress passed the Alien Registration Act, otherwise known as the Smith Act. The Smith Act forbade anyone to "advise, counsel, urge, or in any manner cause insubordination, disloyalty, mutiny, or refusal of duty by any member of the military or naval forces of the United States," and included the prohibition of "any written or printed matter" containing such information. Furthermore, the act made it illegal to advise or teach the "overthrow or destruction of any government in the United States."

The Court reaffirmed the constitutionality of the Smith Act in the 1951 case of *Dennis* versus *the United States*, when it upheld the conviction of eleven leaders of the American Communist Party. Six years later, however, the Court narrowed the act when it said that writing or speaking about overthrowing the government was

A marshal's van heads for jail with several
Communist leaders convicted in 1951 of conspiracy to teach
and advocate the overthrow of the United States government.

protected by the free speech clause of the First Amendment. The justices maintained that it was still illegal to specifically instruct people in such action.

During wartime, the American public has largely been supportive of such censoring measures in the name of national security. Other cases of governmental censorship or attempts to censor, however, have at times posed disturbing questions to the nation's citizens: just how much information should our government be permitted to withhold from us? On the other hand, how much should citizens, including government employees, be permitted to say about "sensitive" topics?

The Marchetti Case

Victor Marchetti was an employee of the Central Intelligence Agency (CIA) of the United States for fourteen years—until September 1969. After leaving the agency, Marchetti, with John Marks, who had worked with the State Department, wrote a book entitled *The CIA and the Cult of Intelligence*. In the book, the authors voiced concerns about the policies of the CIA, and in many instances, they included information about the agency's procedures and history, based upon Marchetti's experiences as an employee.

While working for the agency, Marchetti had signed agreements that forbade him to disclose classified or sensitive information, unless authorized to do so. Marchetti and Marks presented the manuscript of *The CIA and the Cult of Intelligence* to CIA officials for their review prior to its publication. The authors found the results devastating: over 300 passages—a large portion of the book—had been edited out.

A long and difficult legal battle began. Although the number of passages deleted from the book was reduced to 168, the authors argued that the heavy editing was in violation of their First Amendment right to free speech, and that the government must be limited in its powers of censorship over federal employees.

A 1972 federal Court of Appeals decision supported the CIA's position on disallowing the authors to publish the classified information in question. In 1975, the Supreme Court's decision not to review the case closed it permanently, and acknowledged the government's right to secrecy.

Secrecy Agreements

While the outcome of the Marchetti case affirmed the government's ability to censor its employees to some degree, the extent to which it should be able to do this is still far from decided. In the 1980s, the issue of governmental requirements concerning secrecy agreements with federal employees has been the subject of heavy debate.

Shortly after resigning from her position as U.S. ambassador to the United Nations, Jeane Kirkpatrick was asked to sign a prepublication clearance form, which would require her to submit nearly everything she wrote to the State Department for review. Mrs. Kirkpatrick refused to sign the form, recognizing immediately how much this would restrict her writing.

But since 1981, more than 120,000 government employees have signed a lifetime censorship agreement. In March 1983, President Reagan introduced an even stricter policy, which would enable a government administration to censor books, articles, newspaper columns, editorials, letters to the editor, and even fiction written by government employees. Reaction to this directive was so strong that the President placed the policy on hold, yet many government agencies do require such secrecy agreements of their employees.

The Freedom of Information Act

Established in 1967, the Freedom of Information Act permits all citizens access to government information, unless the information falls under special exemption. The first exemption, for example, permits information to be withheld from the public if it is "in the interests of national defense and foreign policy."

The Freedom of Information Act is an important tool for citizens in their effort to remain informed about our government's policies and operations. Recent modifications to this act, however, have narrowed the scope of information available. Under new administration guidelines, more and more information may be placed in the "classified" category, thus making it unavailable to the public.

The Right to Know

The issues of requiring federal employees to sign secrecy agreements and limiting the information available through the Freedom of Information Act are cause for serious study by citizens concerned with preserving our right to be informed. Press censorship, as demonstrated recently in the press "blackout" during the Grenada invasion, poses another dilemma. While many government officials believe that we must guard our national security at any cost, others argue that this is a violation of First Amendment rights, and that, instead, citizens must be permitted to keep a close eye on the government. Measures taken to insure national security must be limited, they argue, when those measures severely conflict with the citizen's right to know.

8

The Right to
Intellectual Freedom

In his biography, *Thomas Jefferson: The Complete Man*, author James A. Eichner describes the following incident which occurred while Jefferson was president:

> A German visitor to the White House saw there a newspaper full of abuse of President Jefferson, and asked why the President did not have the fellow who wrote it hanged. "What? Hang the guardian of the public morals?" asked Jefferson. "Put that paper into your pocket, my good friend," he told the visitor, "and carry it with you to Europe, and when you hear anyone doubt the reality of American freedom, show them that paper, and tell them where you found it."

A leading spokesman for civil liberties, Jefferson was proud of our nation's commitment to protect freedom of expression through the First Amendment to the Constitution. He believed in the "illimitable freedom of the human mind."

The wealth of knowledge available today to all Americans—

Thomas Jefferson, third president of the United States, strongly opposed censorship of expression.

through our schools, universities, libraries, museums, theaters, galleries, and many forms of news and information media—would have pleased Jefferson. We are a curious nation, and continue to grow more knowledgeable about our world and the issues that concern us: domestic and foreign affairs; scientific and technological advances; military arms control; and the problems of crime, poverty, discrimination, and pornography. As concerned citizens, we desire to be able to consume lots of information, and to be able to ask questions and speak freely about the issues.

This desire for knowledge is a sign of a healthy society, but it raises many questions pertaining to the issue of censorship. Our tendency to censor arises from our wish to protect each other from harmful information, but in many instances, who is the best judge if not ourselves?

Many organizations that oppose censorship have developed guidelines to assist teachers, students, librarians, writers, and others to make careful, important distinctions about censorship. These groups stress that the answer to resolving imbalances is not simply the elimination of poor or inadequate information, but the addition of better, more useful information. "Advise, instead of control," recommends the National Council of Teachers of English in its professional guidelines. "Seek to educate, to increase access to ideas and information."

Such an affirmative approach to improving our educational materials and other forms of communication is an important step in shifting away from the potentially dangerous effects of censorship. Without the freedom to read, write, speak, and therefore to think and learn, our society would suffocate and in many ways cease to progress. Instead, the liberties we share in this country, if carefully preserved, will insure that creative and curious minds will never be restrained, nor voices silenced.

For Further Reading

Blanshard, Paul. *The Right To Read: The Battle Against Censorship.* Boston: Beacon Press, 1955.

Freedom of Inquiry: Supporting the Library Bill of Rights. Washington, D.C.: American Library Association, 1965.

Hohenberg, John. *Free Press/Free People: The Best Cause.* New York: Columbia University Press, 1971.

Hoyt, Olga G. and Edwin P. Hoyt. *Censorship in America.* New York: Seabury Press, 1973.

Levy, Leonard W., editor. *Freedom of the Press: From Zenger to Jefferson.* New York: Bobbs-Merrill, 1966.

Snyder, Gerald S. *The Right to Be Informed: Censorship in the United States.* New York: Julian Messner, 1976.

For Further Information

National Council of Teachers of English
111 Kenyon Road
Urbana, IL 61801

Office for Intellectual Freedom
American Library Association
50 East Huron St.
Chicago, IL 60611

P.E.N. American Center
156 Fifth Avenue
New York, NY 10010

People For The American Way
1424 16th St., N.W.
Suite 601
Washington, D.C. 20036

Index